ROCK

WITH

ME

A book of poetry and journaling for growth & reflection.

By Ricky and Valerie Hughes

Rock with Me

copyright © 2020 by Ricky and Valerie Hughes

All rights reserved. No part of this book may be reproduced, distributed, or transmitted in any form or by any means, including photocopying, recording, or other electronic or mechanical methods, without the prior written permission of the publisher, except in the case of brief quotations embodied in critical reviews and certain other noncommercial uses permitted by copyright law.

Business Inquires & Ordering Information:

HuesofRocks.com

Published By: Ricky and Valerie Hughes

Drawing by Hayden Sample

For our children - Create and be kind.

Contents

Money — 1
Twin Mattress — 2
Guap-A-Mole — 4

Social Media — 7
My Space — 8
F Social Media — 10

Loss — 13
Hey Mickey — 14
Mickey Mouse — 18

Legacy — 21
3 — 22
Chilrennn — 26

Mental Health — 29
Mental Budget — 30
Note to Self — 34

Where We're Headed — 47
Rock Steady — 48

Journal — 51

Money

1 | Rock with Me

Twin Mattress
Valerie

I know we deep in love and excited to go half on a baby
But we digging deep in these pockets going half on these bills

Moving in together was cute
His and Her towels, 800 count sheets, matching robes and slippers
We bout to be in for a treat

We hear it now
Rooster crowing, alarm going off, Bone Thugs rapping, *"It's the 1st of tha month!!!"*

But we ain't in perfect harmony
These bills getting crazy, we ain't nothing close to lazy
Imma have to get busy, pick up one more shift and get these tips

We gon have to pay this one late to pay this one on time
And nah, we don't wanna do direct withdrawal
We need to see it come out, in case we gotta rob Peter to pay Paul

Let's gon & skip church today cuz you know they gon pass round the plate
Wishing one of our Mommas call and ask, have we ate?!
We ain't doing bad, we just adjusting
Financial literacy, we just ain't accustomed

Why spend mine when I can spend yours is no longer even a question
Student loans? Don't even mention!!

Truth is, I'd choose penny-pinching with you over rich with someone else
And that's a proven fact

Remember the twin mattress on the studio floor?
We in a queen-size now
You treating me to Queen-Tingz now
Pinch me if I'm dreaming
We headed to California Kinging now

Guap-A-Mole
Ricky

Just thinking about this gives me anxiety, but here goes nothing...

I eat guap-a-mole, I speak guapanese
Guap, Guap, Guap, all a ninja need
Hiyaaaaaaaaaaaaaaaa
Hayden's karate class was like a hundred a month
Broke my key fob, that's a cool hundred to pop my trunk
Mannn, it's always something coming up
If financial literacy was a class, I would have been flunked
I'm like "this close" to looking for change in the couch
Get anxious every time I log into my mobile account
Well I ain't broke, but I'm cracked
Looking for side gigs, trying to stack
A Pescatarian, but how much is that Big Mac?
Income tax season, aww that's that special sauce
We funding this book with that, boss
Just to add that legacy gloss
Done came a long way from stressing
We can pay our bills, that's a blessing
Like Imo's salad with house dressing
That check to check was too redundant

This next chapter, we on abundance
I'm cool on the burger with the cheese
Give me the bread with the hummus
75% of black people are lactose intolerant, that's hard to stomach
Palms itching and I feel it in my stomach
Is your page private or is it public?
Do you do it for the fam or for the Gram?
I know money ain't everything, but the thing is everything cost
We got way too many ideas to be broke
Plan in place, heart in it; that's artichoke
Our kids aren't gonna have to pull themselves up from their bootstraps, that's hella whack
Their boots gotta be laced with double knots
Goodwill 50% off with the green dots
Manifesting big guap
Magnetically attracting with the Law, jackpot
I'm David, broke is Goliath and bread is the slingshot
And you know I have to butter yo biscuit
Dem Vardi B money moves, got us crab legs from fish sticks
For the kids we go all out for Christmas, but YOU are my wish list
Manifesting financial freedom, so optimistic
A million, or a billion, is that success?
Naw, let's digress,
Peace of mind is priceless
Generational Health, now that's Generational Wealth
Now gon dip those chips in that guap-a-mole

5 | Rock with Me

Ricky's Simple but Essentials

- Stop buying unnecessary things & budget every dollar
- Thrift shop, Sale Shop, Goodwill, etc. Need> Want
- Save a certain amount a month and stick to it. 10% of your income is a good start.
- Invest in yourself FIRST. Start a business. Work to fund that business.
- Travel. See the world! It will inspire you!
- Read: *The Richest Man in Babylon* by George S. Clason

Social Media

My Space
Valerie

Been on it for over 10 years
Felt like the only way I could get my space
Used to dial up the connect just to get a taste
I'd be running, man just to hop into a session
If you were trying to call, you ain't getting through cuz I was busy on my own planet
Everything else went black while we lit up
Music playing in the background
Sometimes it was Rap
Sometimes smooth R&B
Sometimes even Gospel
You knew my crew, at least the top 8
Matter of fact, you slid through and we got our first taste of reconnection
I played it cute, trying to save face
But I could've written a whole book on how I felt about you, boy
I was hooked
You were hooked
We shared a similar addiction with different afflictions
We were young, wild, and free
Made plenty of mistakes
At least 140 of them
We were some characters
Thank God we grew, but marriage did not erase those temptations

Try that Yo Gotti shit again as if you don't already have an Angela & I'll go ghost
I'd be lying if I said it still ain't a struggle for me too
Not even sure what to consider being clean
How much of a Gram is too much to take? What if I take a few breaks?
I don't know if I need a prescription or another subscription
Got the nerve to tell you I need some space, hop on the toilet and scroll so long I can't feel my legs
One of the most private daily occurrences, I close the door, shut my family out, and let the world in
I go back and forth on if there are more pros than cons, more gains than sins
On whether I can be a light in a dark place or if that's even my calling
I love it for the outlet it can be
And the connection it can bring
As long as I'm plugged into my Source, I can shine & navigate through anything

F Social Media
Ricky

Just thinking about this gives me anxiety, but here goes nothing...

So much on my mind, it be hard to rewind
So much on my heart, I don't know where to start
I came from a time where either I'll call you on your house phone or I'd meet you at the skating rink
Wasn't no wyd or brb
Now, I could be laying in my bed and still see you at the skating rink
A big illusion that I have fallen victim to, two thousand too many times
As I scroll down nothing but comparisons and temptations
Either leaves me deflated or doing something I would have never contemplated
Because of this dumb thumb, I'm regretting and deleting
But it doesn't disappear
It's still there
That scroll can take a tole
Gotta get control
Damn, I hate Instagram
But man, I love Instagram
I wish social media was never created
I can't live without it though

I'm not addicted
I delete my app
Next day I'm right back
It can either be a foundation for a big mistake
Or the platform for a big break
Trying to navigate my anxiety cause I gotta message
I got something to say
I done came a long way
GPS needs better signal as I navigate
I need boundaries
I need me time
Without y'all time
Hit send, anxious algorithm is the price
Post a pic with Val, gon double my likes
The Rock in DMs, that's royal rumble with wife
A thin line between cyber and real
No separation causes damage
Common sense is absent; down that rabbit hole like Alice
Battling the old me like Cassius
Let's just delete our pages and move to Dallas
And start a #LoveYouInANewCityChallenge
Reporting Live from balance
Instagram,
Therapy
Facebook,
Meditation
YouTube,
Pray..
Log off!

Ricky's Simple but Essentials

- Unfollow Everyone. Then refollow only the people that add value to your life (No Using the Explore Page on the Gram)
- Use social media no more than 4 days a week (Unless special occasion). The days you are not on social media, delete the apps from your phone.
- Spend Time Alone (Solitude) & with "Framily" (Solidarity).
- Revisit or Find a Hobby
- Take a full week off social media once every 4 months.
- Read at least 1 book a month.
- Read: *Digital Minimalism* by Cal Newport

Loss

Hey Mickey
Valerie

I owe you
What you carried, birthed, nurtured, raised,
and love saved me
Raised me emotionally
We joked about you cutting the cord, but I'm
glad you ain't give a damn
See that's my man, but he's your seed
Something I could never and would never
want to come between
You did the damn thing
Without a Google search, Pinterest, or
YouTube
You knew to pour love and affection into your
kids
You raised a black man
You raised a black man
He ain't afraid to say sorry
Ain't ashamed to say he loves me
And even though he might bottle it up, when
the time's right, he'll let his emotions show
Our pillow talk is about triggers and seasonal
depression
How even though he didn't feel like getting
out the bed, he got up to go to his therapist
We on some whole heal your trauma shit
But you are the one that planted that seed

Your own struggles taught him valuable lessons that otherwise would've taken a lifetime to learn
Like journal, write your pain down
Ask God for help
But know that you can help yourself
It's okay to be angry, but forgive quickly
I never met anyone who could do either of those like you
Cuss somebody out and be ready to fight
But be the first to genuinely apologize to someone you loved
I wish he; I wish we didn't lose you in the flesh
It felt like you were wrongfully taken from us
It felt like God hated us
The timing still doesn't feel right
I had never felt so afraid or unprepared in my life
Breaths sound different when you counting them
Those moments changed us forever
Watching him lose his very best friend
You talking about breaking a man
Why did God take you, man?!
I wish I could take all his pain
Truth is, I don't know what to do with mine
But I'd take his no question
I didn't know how to say it then, but I better understand now
I was in shock, traumatized, and living in fear

15 | Rock with Me

If you were his heartbeat, what's to keep his beating
I wish I could've said that out loud then
But I got just 2 days of bereavement
We had a son to raise, bills to pay, a house to clean
Life was moving on without saying sorry
That helped and hurt simultaneously
"*Sorry for your loss*" sounds like a momentarily apology as if this grief is not on-going
I see it in his face when he realizes he's still losing you
I cherish the days when we feel you
I love the days when we smile and laugh thinking about you
You are close
The love you have for your kids is beyond this lifetime
If there are two sets of footprints in the sand during his saddest moments, I wouldn't be surprised
Thank God for carrying him
And you for staying right by his side
I love you, Mickey
I owe you

17 | Rock with Me

Mickey Mouse
Ricky

Just thinking about this gives me anxiety, but here goes nothing...

Mickey Mickey Bo Bickey Bananafana Fo Fickey, Fee Fi Mo Mickey, Mickeeeeyyyyy
Gotta laugh to keep from crying
Gotta live to keep from dying
But first, thank you for showing me the meaning of unconditional LOVE!
I ain't been the same since April 7th, 2015
Like 7 hours earlier we were laughing together drinking red zinger tea
You know, just how you liked it; hella lemon, hella sugar
It was late and I had to leave
You grabbed me and gave me hella sugar
You was like, "Ricky, just stay the night"
I'm like, "Momma, I got a whole wife"
We hugged and I dipped
The last time I felt your lips
It looked like I was holding up so well
But inside I was living hell
Depressed, Capital D
Even when I found out Val was pregnant, it was bittersweet
All I could think of was NO Grandma Michelle for my baby and me

I was an invisible tornado
Spiraling out of control, but nobody knew
I ain't gonna front, most of the time I push you to the back of my mind
That's how I cope
Times when I feel like not being here anymore
I feel your energy
You and God created this synergy
You were the only person that made me feel like I could do anything
You told me Val was the one when I was a blind fool
On the 4th of July we danced to Stevie Wonder, them fireworks flew
You broke down when I dropped out of Mizzou
You gon' be too hype though cause I'm about to graduate from SLU
Who knew?
People still say I act just like you
Damn
We ain't got Michelle Flowers
But we got Harlow Flower-Ann Hughes
I love you Mickey!

Ricky's Simple but Essentials

- Be kind always, to everyone and you will have no regrets.
- Find your "New Normal".
- It's okay to be weak because God will give you strength. (Thanks, Yolanda.)
- Keep breathing. Big, Deep Breaths.
- Talk about it. Grieve. Cry. Scream. Do not hold it in.
- "Make Yo Momma Proud!!"

Legacy

3
Valerie

Forever
Forever grateful
Forever love

I lost myself in you
But I found myself too

I changed
I rearranged
I made space where there was none

I cried hidden tears
I lost unseen battles that I have the scars to prove

I went toe to toe with depression
In ways, it killed me
In other ways, resurrected

Forever
Forever grateful
Forever love

I can't go back to who I was
And I don't want to

Make time for self-love
At times it is solely so I can love you better

This is the safest place for love this deep
Love this profound
And even though it comes with some pain and heartbreak
I dig deeper

Forever
Forever grateful
Forever love

Happiness and joy do not do this feeling justice
I am elated
I am fulfilled
I am walking in my purpose

Raising you
Growing with you
Understanding my past so I can be more tender toward you

Forever
Forever grateful
Forever love

3 knows the best version of me
The learner and the teacher
The lover and the protector
The calmness and the storm
The hurt and the healed
And still inspires me to be greater

2 challenged me
Exposed the imbalance in me
Provided clarity I did not know I was missing
Gifted us with a necessary peace and motivation

1 deserves to feel the significance that comes with that number
New beginnings, new life, alpha
I was young and imperfect
But you always came first
Forgive me for not understanding mental health
I was who I was
Now I am who I am, and I am grateful I get to share her with you

Forever
Forever grateful
Forever love

I can accept that most things in this world don't belong to me
But The 3 feel different

I understand you are your own beings with
your own journeys
But you are every bit of me
You live in me
I live in you
What do you call legacy in the reverse?
I am inheriting from you
Wisdom
Patience
Abundance
Unconditional love
Superpowers
Mental and spiritual wealth

I am passing that back through you
Know early on, you are assigned to you
Love and take care of yourself
Be in tune with self
Be your purpose
Be humble, but don't play small
Treat people kindly
Make the world better
When you need help, ask for it
Sit with your beauty and see the beauty in
others

Be
Forever
Forever grateful
Forever love

Chilrennn
Ricky

Just thinking about this gives me anxiety, but here goes nothing...

I said in a song *"I love Hayden like my own son, and if his asthma act up, he could have both lungs."*
6 years later I would probably say, *"I love my son Hayden, but if his asthma is acting up, he better have his albuterol cause we teach love and responsibility, dude"*
What's crazy is he is the closest thing to a grandkid my Momma ever knew
Well kinda, because Momma, Harlow is you
And Violet, well we still trying to figure her out
Shoot, I'm still trying to figure it all out
Like being a husband and a father
Being a black husband and father
I never had a mentor or a role model that lead
Everything I learned is from bumping my head
Daddy issues, blaming him for things I didn't know
I got my own kids now, I gotta breathe in slow
I gotta let that go

See in a 5-minute span I can go from changing a diaper
To teaching ABC's
To helping with Algebraaa....BRUH!
Used to be a migraine, now it's my gain
The unconditional love is hard to explain
Like when it's 90 degrees, but it still rains
Umbrella like protection when life gets hurricane
Some days I got Buddha brain, some days I'm Charlamagne
But errrday them crazy kids keep me sane
And y'all momma!? THE BEST IN THE WORLD. No cap but ALL CAPS
The intuitive nature she has, it should be her next book
Ain't enough pages in this one to express how you saved my life
Time is flying
I just pray I get it right
Tragedy is terrifying
This I pray every night
Lord, protect my wife
Lord, protect my kids
Lord, protect my kids' kids' kids
Amen

Ricky's Simple but Essentials

- Treat spending time with your kids like it's your OWN time.
- It is okay to make mistakes. It is also necessary to apologize to your kids when you make mistakes. Learn and apply.
- Hug them, kiss them, tell them you love them even when they get on your nerves. Cherish them.
- Do not compare them to each other or to other people's kids.
- Live in the "Now" but prepare for the future. *Life Insurance*
- Learn by trial and error aka I haven't found "This" book yet.

Mental Health

Mental Budget
Valerie

I survived Postpartum Depression 3 times, 2 times unknowingly
That's not a statement of pride
I could've died
Young black girl knew nothing of mental health
Knew little of taking care of self
14 years ago, the only thing that got checked on me was my cervix after 6 weeks
No emotional check for the black girl that did it to herself
No ask of suicidal thoughts, I had em even pre-partum
I wish I could say I thought about any of that then, but this ain't nothing but reflection
10 and 12 years later, some of it would happen again
How was I supposed to know the difference between baby blues and depression?
The difference between being worried about my kids and being internally anxious most the time?
I worked tirelessly and complained endlessly to keep the house clean
Just to make my loss of energy make sense, just to give me something to control

They say breast is best, but I couldn't have been more stressed
Pumping to keep up my supply
Would've switched to formula, but that wasn't in the budget
See numbers are my trigger too
Leaving a light on when no one's home feels like taking food out my babies' mouths
Oddly enough, Postpartum Depression and the things that set me off were my catalyst to help me understand and take care of myself mentally
If I don't have it to give, I don't give it
If I have it to give, I calculate if it's a smart investment
Meaning I stack up my emotional savings account and withdraw when needed
Knowing I am going to have to pay myself back whether that's through my own doing or others
When I need a loan, I look to ones I trust
I've received advances from my husband, a counselor, my sisters, my Momma, and friends
We all are just trying to make these ends
Never knowing what life is gonna throw at us
I often wonder if the apple didn't fall far from the tree
There's no way this pain started with me
Even the weight of that about kills me
Knowing the people, I love most feel this too
I can't help but to drop to one knee

31 | Rock with Me

Please give us a hand
Either reverse the curse or help us all to see each other as human
Amen
Gratitude to my Mother and Grandmother
For the battles seen and unseen
Your love and sacrifice help me understand myself better
If I'm every woman, it's because you live in me
So, I am saying grace before eating meals that are good for my body and brain
I am exercising regularly
I am praying and meditating to help keep my mind right
Intimacy with my husband is just as important as intimacy with myself
Planning is my gift, but I never have the ultimate say
Truth is some shit just happens without our consent
Furthermore understanding
God, grant me the serenity to accept that I am doing my best
And the courage to believe everyone else is doing the same

33 | Rock with Me

Note to Self
Ricky

Just thinking about this give me anxiety, but here goes nothing...

First, I do not have all the answers
This is something that I deal with everyday
Pastor like, go pray
Mouth moving but didn't know what to say
Young, Black, and Depressed
As I look back on my life it's been a decade of mess
No talk in my community about mental health
I chalked it up to stress

Trauma on trauma
PTSD, shot at a few times, wrecked a few cars, drinking, drugs, drugs, drinking, Dee-Dee died, Granny died, Aunties died, Momma died, doubt, fear, struggling husband, not loving myself, suicidal thoughts, et cetera, et cetera, spiraling out of control..
Head on a swivel, dodging my people and the po-po
I'm steady taking bones out my closet, one by one
Never dealt with nothing inside
But I had them new J's with them 20's on my ride

Nobody knew I was ready to die
The gift of the present was about to get returned with no refund
My life was on lay-a-way and I was broke as a joke
Regrets plague my mental then comes rumination
Keep playing that same thought over and over and over
Like I know how it's gonna end...bad
Catastrophizing
Sheer terror
Val, please forgive me for all my errors
Dying inside, she was my pallbearer
Young, Black, and Depressed with nobody to talk to
After that one breakdown then I knew...
I NEED HELP
Googled therapist in the Lou
Went through a few
Started meditating out the blue
Started reading books that changed my life
Inconsistent journaling, but still got me right
I started working out and *"woo"*
I could think a little more clear
Why did it take me 20 years to get here?
Cause they don't talk about mental health where I'm from
Don't get it twisted, my mind still be twisted
Dreadlock, brain in headlock

If you down, Homie like fire up then
When you frown, Bro like pour up then
When you spinning round, Cuz like where the chicks at?
Is it me or is it in my family tree?
Either way I gotta take care of myself
I gotta love myself, I have to forgive myself
God must have heard my prayer, huh?
Thank God for Therapy
Thank God for Mediation
Thank God for Books
Thank God for my random journals
Thank God for the time and ability to get my a$$ out the bed and work out
Thank God for my family who loves me unconditionally
I don't have all the answers, but I do know this
Life is hard
Take it second by second, minute by minute, day by day
I might be good today
Tomorrow not so much
No rush, just get through
First take care of you
Young, Black, and Depressed but
Young, Black, and Blessed
Young, Black, and Doing my Best
You are worthy, you deserve joy
You can get through
Take care of YOU
Note to Self

Ricky's Simple but Essentials

- Talk to someone, get a counselor, or get a therapist.
- Mediate. It is not easy but try a little every day. It gets easier. It is amazing.
- Exercise: Walk, jog, run, lift weights, jumping jacks, Yoga, Zumba, etc.
- Read a book! Then read another! Then read another!
- Journal every day or every other day!
- When life gets tough, up your self-care. You deserve it.
- Read: *Meditations* by Marcus Aurelius

Reunited at a Mizzou College Party *2008*

Free Date to the Zoo *2008*

In the Deez Beats Studio (Twin Mattress not pictured) *August 2008*

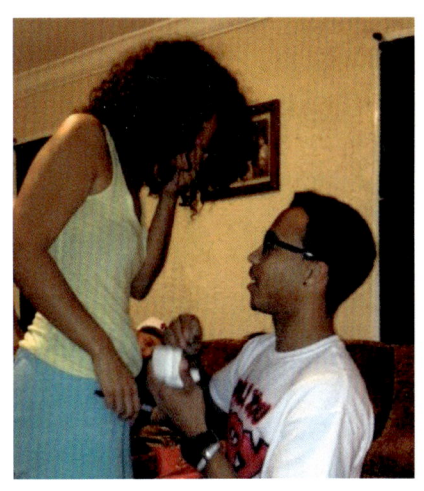

Our Engagement November *2015*

39 | Rock with Me

Our Wedding Day *July 4, 2014*

Val picking up "one mo shift to get these tips" while being visited by our amazing son
January 2015

Ricky in Ferguson, MO
RIP Mike Brown *2015*

40 | Rock with Me

Like Momma, Like Daughter *1990*

Val & her Grandma Valeria.
Namesake *2002*

Val's Siblings: Traci, Alexis,
Blake, Troy, & Lindsay

Martin Family *2018*

Ricky's Beautiful Momma, Michelle Jean Flowers-Hughes
2/13/1950 – 4/7/2015

Mickey & Ricky with Santa aka Uncle Tony *1988*

Mickey with her babies, Ricky & Leslie *1989*

The Flowers Family: Linda, Donielle, Michelle, Leslie, Grandma Helen, Sydney, Ricky, Tony, & Kerry

At our Surprise Engagement Party with Ricky's Parents
2015

Our Wedding Day
July 2014

The Hughes Family on Christmas
2014

Our 3 November 2019

The Simpsons Rockin' Halloween 2019

Baby Hayden 2006

Engagement Pics 2014

44 | Rock with Me

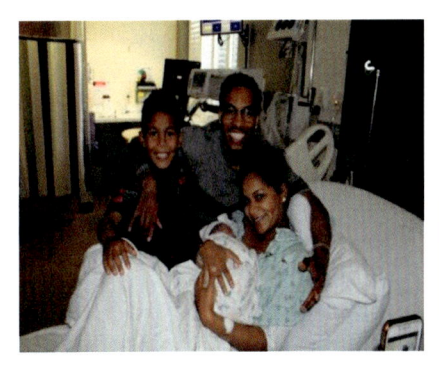

Family of 4. Hi Harlow!
May 2016

Big Brother & Baby Sister
May 2016

Hi Violet! Family of 5!
April 2018

Our 3 Babies November 2018

"It's The Rocks!!" December 2019

45 | Rock with Me

Rock with Me Photo Shoot 2020

46 | Rock with Me

Where We're Headed

Rock Steady
Ricky & Valerie

R: Ayo...so where we headed?

V: Like they say, you don't know where you're going til you know where you've been

R: Well, we been to hell and back and probably going back again

V: Been there 9 times, also kissed Cloud 10

R: But I made mistakes deserving a one-hitter quitter to the chin; in a dark place, talking hanging on by a limb

V: Meanwhile, I'm in shadows all my own still throwing 'bows with my tongue
See saying "I love you" in words is a major accomplishment for me
But showing "I love you" with my words is my shortcoming

R: It's a thin line between coming up short and going the distance
When you get behind, do you quit, or do you finish?

V: The answer is we rockin'
This is different
Breaking generational curses on purpose

R: Eating celery; growing salary
Strawberry in the blender; family blended
Wedding vows; A I O U my errthang vowels

V: This love ain't as easy as 123, but I got you and you got me

R: And for that I gotta thank G.O.D cause you my D.O.G

V: Let's get clear about our goals

R: Get in the best shape of our life…we in the gym getting swole

V: Loving vulnerably and striving to turn the fear of loving then losing a positive black man into the fuel that makes me love you more tender, appreciate you further

R: Fulfilling our purpose to create
Aiming to make the world a better place
Even when we gone, we still hurr

V: We are bringing the village back
Our kids aren't starting from scratch

R&V: And we just scratching the surface

R: Today we might be lit like a rocket and tomorrow we might hit rock bottom

V: Through the highs and the lows, stay ten toes and when life gets hard as a rock just

R&V: Rock with Me!

Journal for Reflection & Growth

"We delight in the beauty of the butterfly, but rarely admit the changes it has gone through to achieve that beauty."

– Maya Angelou

Write down 5 Moments that have impacted your life.

_____

_____

_____

_____

_____

_____

_____

_____

_____

_____

_____

_____

Share these moments with someone you rock with!

Write down 5 Lessons you have learned from these moments.

_____

_____

_____

_____

_____

_____

_____

_____

_____

_____

Share these lessons with someone you rock with!

Write down 5 Positive Affirmations about yourself.

_____

_____

_____

_____

_____

_____

_____

_____

_____

_____

_____

_____

Spend 5 Minutes Every Morning Reflecting on These Affirmations! Say Them Out Loud!

Write down 5 Things you are grateful for and why.

_____

_____

_____

_____

_____

_____

_____

_____

_____

_____

_____

Spend 5 Minutes Every Night Reflecting on the Things You Are Grateful For.

Write down 5 Ways you will use your creativity to fulfill your purpose.

_____

_____

_____

_____

_____

_____

_____

_____

_____

_____

Know and Believe that Your Purpose is to Create!
Rock with yourself!

Write down 5 Characteristics you desire in your partner or future partner.

_____

_____

_____

_____

_____

_____

_____

_____

_____

_____

_____

You deserve the best!

Write down 5 Areas of Opportunities that can help you to be a better partner.

_____
_____
_____
_____
_____
_____
_____
_____
_____
_____
_____
_____
_____
_____

Life is a journey. You are constantly growing into who you are meant to be!

Use the next few pages to journal and reflect on whatever your heart desires.

61 | Rock with Me

63 | Rock with Me

KEEP

ROCKIN'!